Leaving Home

DAVID FRENCH

Introduction by Urjo Kareda

New Drama 7
General Editor: Brian Parker

new press Toronto 1972

Rights to produce this play, in whole or in part, in any medium by any group, amateur or professional, are retained by the author, and interested persons are requested to apply for permission, and for terms to:
    Sage Productions
    Tarragon Theatre
    30 Bridgman Avenue
    Toronto, Ontario

ISBN 0-88770-712-2 cloth
ISBN 0-88770-713-0 paper

First printing.

123456   77   76   75   74   73   72

new press
Order Department
553 Richmond Street West
Toronto 133, Ontario

Photography, Hugh Travers
Design, Pamela Patrick
Typeset by Academic, Professional and Scholarly Publishing Services, Ltd.
Printed by Hunter Rose Co., Toronto
Manufactured in Canada

INTRODUCTION

David French's *Leaving Home* arrived in Toronto near the end of the remarkable 1971–1972 season, a span of theatrical activity during which, creatively, all hell had broken loose. A common subconscious barrier had somehow been lifted, releasing forces which transformed our theatrical character. In the course of that season, there were no less than four theatres constantly offering original Canadian works in Toronto: Theatre Passe Muraille, Factory Theatre Lab, Tarragon Theatre and, arriving for the summer, Toronto Free Theatre. When one adds the occasional Canadian works presented at Toronto Workshop Productions and the Global Village, assorted independent productions, the performances of the travelling Creation 2 ensemble, and even the two Canadian works at the St. Lawrence Centre (pricked more by publicity than conscience, but no matter), the total climbed to well over fifty—over fifty new Canadian plays received full premiere productions in Toronto during that magic launching year.

An atypical unity of purpose was established by affirming the political, moral, and aesthetic necessity of examining and developing our own drama. From there, the explosion of new theatre shot out with extraordinary centrifugal force. Complementary flourishes attended the revolution. The Playwrights Co-op marched in to mass-publish reasonable production scripts, and the federal government's Local Initiatives Program provided financial backing for a number of independent productions.

The swift advance of new drama was specifically related to the rise of new theatres in Toronto which provided an alternative to the unadventurous range of reheated Broadway desserts at Toronto's two commercial theatres. It was as if a dervish of national consciousness had gone through the streets promising 'new theatres for old!' Realizing that a characterless theatre cannot hope to survive, these new theatres quickly created for themselves individual images, often simply a reflection of the man in charge. By logical attraction, certain playwrights gravitated automatically to certain theatres, seeking a mutually satisfying relationship of interests and methods. In the 1971–1972 season, almost all the new plays written were directed toward one of three alternative theatres.

The oldest, Paul Thompson's Theatre Passe Muraille, can be expected to present productions with an idiomatic physical profile emphasizing easily manoeuvred acting areas and performing forces. Collective creation—the preparation of an authorless production, with the actors creating the material out of their own experience or research—has its happiest home at the Passe Muraille. It is a theatre uniquely congenial to both creative directors and authors with directorial obsessions. Two of its most important achievements during the 1971–1972 season emerged from the influence of powerful, visually-oriented directors upon works whose energy is not released verbally: Louis del Grande's production of Hrant Alianuk's *Tantrums*, and John Palmer's production of the Fabian Jennings-Allan Rae collaboration *Charles Manson a.k.a. Jesus Christ*.

At the Factory Theatre Lab, directed by Ken Gass, there is a perpetual aura of work-in-progress. The Factory pioneered the process of regular workshop productions: the urgency of producing as many plays as possible and the right of a young playwright to learn through production are unquestioned impulses. As a result, new works like John Palmer's *A Touch of God in the Golden Age*, Larry Fineberg's *Stonehenge Trilogy*, and George Walker's *Sacktown Rag* are thrust before the public perhaps one or two revisions prematurely. The lowest common denominator of young Canadian playwrights' problems is their lack of experience, an unfamiliarity with the relationship between page and stage inevitable in a culture which hasn't developed its own theatre. The Factory's assembly of raw talents is both a manifestation of this difficulty and its solution.

The emphasis at Bill Glassco's Tarragon Theatre is on editorial assistance for the writer, so that he can develop and polish his material until it is ready for production. An active, persistent collaboration between writer and director, modified by the practical intervention of the actors, examines nuances of structure, dialogue and physical detail. It is no accident, then, that Glassco's productions of David Freeman's *Creeps* and David French's *Leaving Home*—estimable also for their theatrical authority and beauty—provided the most viable scripts of the season purely as written documents. In some cases this personal attention to scripts still produced plays of minimal effectiveness, but the harrowing process of rewriting provided the young writers with insights into the complexities of their craft.

Over fifty new Canadian plays in one season—a phenomenon of quantity is not necessarily a phenomenon of quality. This sudden rampage of original dramatic writing in Toronto had the characteristics of a fervently committed, even possessed, centipede with an instinct for advancing but whose many limbs each possessed an individual artistic vision of its own. Countless dramatic forms were approached, embraced, abandoned. There was a profusion of familiar and mannered forms filtered through films and television, as well as echoes of specific playwrights: the wane of neo-Pinterism is not yet due. It was as if, compressed into one season, we were witnessing a ritualized recreation of the history of modern drama, all-encompassing if not chronological. Vast-scaled epic drama: Louis Capson's technological trilogy *The True North Blueprint* and John Palmer's uncompleted trilogy *Memories for My Brother*. Expressionism: Raymond Canale's *The Jingo Ring*. Documentary drama: *Bethune! Bethune!* and Carol Bolt's *Buffalo Jump*. Historical epic: Rick Salutin's *Fanshen*, from William Hinton's study of the Chinese revolution. Broadway farce: Louis del Grande's *Maybe We Could Get Some Bach*. Happening: Frank Powley and Jim Garrard's *The Black Queen is Going to Eat You All Up*. And a wide selection of absurdist drama: Larry Fineberg's *Stonehenge Trilogy*, James Blumer's *Surd Sandwich* and Sheldon Rosen's *The Wonderful World of William Bends (Who is Not Quite Himself Today)*.

If indeed this interesting season was an unconscious, formal re-enactment of the development of contemporary theatre, then those playwrights who began at the beginning—with naturalism —were the winners. Is it a coincidence that the most fully satisfying, the most finished new plays of the season were all naturalistic in technique: David Freeman's *Creeps*, Bill Fruet's *Wedding in White*, Larry Kardish's *Brussels Sprouts* and David French's *Leaving Home*? Naturalism leads to a useful self-discipline in terms of the material for drama; it suggests, but doesn't impose, an author's response to his experience, a method of transforming personally observed information into an artistic order. (Is it another coincidence that each of these four plays arises from personal history?) Not all the considerable amount of autobiographical writing this season was naturalistic, however: John Palmer's *A Touch of God in the Golden Age*, heavily influenced by Albee, spun itself into a verbal ritual, while George Walker's *Sacktown Rag* was a pastiche of theatrical and cinematic clichés.

Perhaps the poetic quality of naturalism has been underrated. It has certainly been the achievement of Freeman, Fruet, Kardish and French to reawaken audiences to the mysterious richness of the naturalistic technique. Films and documentary television have robbed the theatre of any claim to naturalistic authenticity. What remains, as well as what we understand now about traditional naturalism, is the much more interesting technique of selective naturalism, with the detail carefully gauged and controlled for a poetic resonance. Far from being duplication, naturalism is an impressionistic method with strict and fascinating formal controls.

These four playwrights share a piercing strength of observation. David Freeman has experienced the cruel humiliation of those whose physical handicaps thrust them beyond society, and the grim, savage humour developed in response. Bill Fruet recalls the desperation, the hopelessness, the isolation of life in a remote rural community. Larry Kardish sees the tenuousness of young friendships which cannot survive the challenges of time and self-interest. David French offers us a difficult world of deflected hopes and blocked affections in a family transplanted far from home, far from itself.

The strength of that revolutionary 1971–1972 season lay with old-fashioned, naturalistic drama, unaccountably considered archaic and unworkable. In new drama, it is the most difficult form to master because it requires reserves of self-discipline. It is heartening that some of the best young writers are willing to commit themselves to a style which must, to many, seem virtually primitive. Perhaps the reward lies in the intensity of public response. Toronto audiences were profoundly affected by these plays, which were political only in the crucial sense that they explored the relationships of men, and nationalistic only in the sense that they sprang from, and now have returned to, a specifically Canadian experience. In *Leaving Home*, David French handles the form with great maturity, confidence and honesty; nothing is generalized, everything is specific, and yet from a personal reminiscence comes a universal—dare I say national?—experience. Because he doesn't lie, David French has found a way to speak to us all.

Urjo Kareda

BIOGRAPHICAL NOTES

David French was born January 18, 1939, in Coley's Point, New-foundland. When he was six years old his family moved to Toronto. He attended Rawlinson Public School, Harbord Collegiate and Oakwood Collegiate. After graduation, he studied acting in Toronto under various teachers and at the Pasadena Playhouse in California. For several years he worked as an actor, as well as a deckhand, janitor, night watchman, postal clerk, apricot picker, and shipper in a ball-point pen factory.

He sold his first one-act play, *Beckons the Dark River*, to the C.B.C. in 1963, and switched from acting to writing. Since then he has written several short stories, one of which, *A Change of Heart*, was published in *The Montrealer*; an unpublished novel, *A Company of Strangers*; and numerous scripts for radio and television. *Leaving Home* is his first full-length stage play, and he is currently at work on his second.

CHRONOLOGY OF PLAYS AND WORKS FOR
RADIO AND TELEVISION

1963   *Beckons the Dark River*—produced on C.B.C. Television 1963, not published

1964   *The Willow Harp*—produced on C.B.C. Television 1964, not published

1964   *A Ring for Florie*—produced on C.B.C. Television 1964, not published

1965   *After Hours*—produced on C.B.C. Television 1965, not published

1965   *Sparrow on a Monday Morning*—produced on C.B.C. Television 1965, and on Philadelphia E.T.V. 1966, not published

1967   *Angeline*—produced on C.B.C. Radio 1967, not published

1967   *Invitation to a Zoo*—produced on C.B.C. Radio 1967, not published

1968   *The Winter of Timothy*—produced on C.B.C. Radio 1968, not published

1970   *A Token Gesture*—produced on C.B.C. Television 1970, not published

1972   *The Happiest Man in the World*—adaptation of the Hugh Garner short story; produced on C.B.C. Television 1972, not published

1972   *Leaving Home*—produced 1972, printed this edition*

This play is lovingly dedicated
to my parents, who were there,
and to Leslie, who wasn't.

Leaving Home

ACKNOWLEDGEMENT

I would like to express
sincere thanks to Bill Glassco
for his help in the development
of this play.

LEAVING HOME was first performed May 16, 1972 at the Tarragon Theatre, Toronto, with the following cast:

MARY MERCER	Maureen Fitzgerald
BEN MERCER	Frank Moore
BILLY MERCER	Mel Tuck
JACOB MERCER	Sean Sullivan
KATHY JACKSON	Lyn Griffin
MINNIE JACKSON	Liza Creighton
HAROLD	Les Carlson

Directed by Bill Glassco
Designed by Dan Yarhi and Stephen Katz
Costumes by Vicky Manthorpe

SCENE

The play is set in Toronto on an early November day in the late fifties.

ACT ONE

The lights come up on a working-class house in Toronto. The stage is divided into three playing areas: kitchen, dining room, and living room. In addition there is a hallway leading into the living room. Two bedroom doors lead off the hallway, as well as the front door which is offstage.

The kitchen contains a fridge, a stove, cupboards over the sink for everyday dishes, and a small drop-leaf table with two wooden chairs, one at either end. A plastic garbage receptacle stands beside the stove. A hockey calendar hangs on a wall, and a kitchen prayer.

The dining room is furnished simply with an oak table and chairs. There is an oak cabinet containing the good dishes and silverware. Perhaps a family portrait hangs on the wall—a photo taken when the sons were much younger.

The living room contains a chesterfield and an armchair, a T.V., a record player and a fireplace. On the mantle rests a photo album and a silver-framed photo of the two sons—then small boys—astride a pinto pony. On one wall hangs a mirror. On another, a seascape. There is also a small table with a telephone on it.

It is around five-thirty on a Friday afternoon, and MARY MER-CER, aged fifty, stands before the mirror in the living room, admiring her brand new dress and fixed hair. As she preens, the front door opens and in walk her two sons, BEN, eighteen, and BILL, seventeen. Each carries a box from a formal rental shop and schoolbooks.

MARY
Did you bump into your father?

BEN

No, we just missed him, Mom. He's already picked up his tux. He's probably at the Oakwood. *(He opens the fridge and helps himself to a beer.)*

MARY

Get your big nose out of the fridge. And put down that beer. You'll spoil your appetite.

BEN

No, I won't. *(He searches for a bottle opener in a drawer.)*

MARY

And don't contradict me. What other bad habits you learned lately?

BEN

(teasing) Don't be such a grouch. You sound like Dad. *(He sits at the table and opens his beer.)*

MARY

Yes, well just because you're in university now, don't t'ink you can raid the fridge any time you likes.

BILL crosses the kitchen and throws his black binder and books in the garbage receptacle.

MARY

What's that for? *(BILL exits into his bedroom and she calls after him.)* It's not the end of the world, my son. *(pause)* Tell you the truth, Ben. We always figured you'd be the one to land in trouble, if anyone did. I don't mean that as an insult. You're more . . . I don't know . . . like your father.

BEN

I am?

Music from BILL's room.

MARY

(calling, exasperated) Billy, do you have to have that so loud? *(BILL turns down his record player. To BEN)* I'm glad your graduation went okay last night. How was Billy? Was he glad he went?

BEN

Well, he wasn't upset, if that's what you mean.

MARY

(slight pause) Ben, how come you not to ask your father?

BEN

What do you mean?

BILL

(off) Mom, will you pack my suitcase? I can't get everything in.

MARY

(calling) I can't now, Billy. Later.

BEN

I want to talk to you, Mom. It's important.

MARY

I want to talk to you, too.

BILL

(Comes out of bedroom, crosses to kitchen.) Mom, here's the deposit on my locker. I cleaned it out and threw away all my old gym clothes. *(He helps himself to an apple from the fridge.)*

MARY

Didn't you just hear me tell your brother to stay out of there? I might as well talk to the sink. Well, you can t'row away your old school clothes—that's your affair—but take those books out of the garbage. Go on. You never knows. They might come in handy sometime.

BILL

How? *(He takes the books out, then sits at the table with BEN.)*

MARY

Well, you can always go to night school and get your senior matric, once the baby arrives and Kathy's back to work. . . . Poor child. I talked to her on the phone this morning. She's still upset, and I don't blame her. I'd be hurt myself if my own mother was too drunk to show up to my shower.

BILL

(a slight ray of hope) Maybe she won't show up tonight.

MARY

(Glances anxiously at the kitchen clock and turns to check the fish and potatoes.) Look at the time. I just wish to goodness he had more t'ought, your father. The supper'll dry up if he don't hurry. He might pick up a phone and mention when he'll be home. Not a grain of t'ought in his head. And I wouldn't put it past him to forget his tux in the beer parlour. *(Finally she turns and looks at her two sons, disappointed.)* And look at the two of you. Too busy with your mouths to give your mother a second glance. I could stand here till my legs dropped off before either of you would notice my dress.

BEN

It's beautiful, Mom.

MARY

That the truth?

BILL

Would we lie to you, Mom?

MARY

Just so long as I don't look foolish next to Minnie. She can afford to dress up—Willard left her well off when he died.

BEN
Don't worry about the money. Dad won't mind.

MARY
Well, it's not every day your own son gets married, is it? *(to BILL as she puts on large apron)* It's just that I don't want Minnie Jackson looking all decked out like the *Queen Mary* and me the tug that dragged her in. You understands, don't you, Ben?

BEN
Sure.

BILL
I understand too, Mom.

MARY
I know you do, Billy. I know you do. *(She opens a tin of peaches and fills five dessert dishes.)* Minnie used to go with your father. Did you know that, Billy? Years and years ago.

BILL
No kidding?

BEN
(at the same time) Really?

MARY
True as God is in Heaven. Minnie was awful sweet on Dad, too. She t'ought the world of him.

BILL
(incredulously) Dad?

MARY
Don't act so surprised. Your father was quite a one with the girls.

BEN
No kidding?

MARY

He could have had his pick of any number of girls. *(to BILL)* You ask Minnie sometime. Of course, in those days I was going with Jerome McKenzie, who later became a Queen's Counsel in St. John's. I must have mentioned him.

The boys exchange smiles.

BEN

I think you have, Mom.

BILL

A hundred times.

MARY

(gently indignant—to BILL) And that I haven't!

BILL

She has too. Hasn't she, Ben?

MARY

Never you mind, Ben. *(to BILL)* And instead of sitting around gabbing so much you'd better go change your clothes. Kathy'll soon be here. *(as BILL crosses to his bedroom)* Is the rehearsal still at eight?

BILL

We're supposed to meet Father Douglas at the church at five to. I just hope Dad's not too drunk. *(He exits.)*

MARY

(Studies BEN a moment.) Look at yourself. A cigarette in one hand, a bottle of beer in the other, at your age! You didn't learn any of your bad habits from me, I can tell you. *(pause)* Ben, don't be in such a hurry to grow up. *(She sits across from him.)* Whatever you do, don't be in such a hurry. Look at your poor young brother. His whole life ruined. Oh, I could weep a bellyful when I t'inks of it. Just seventeen, not old enough to sprout

whiskers on his chin, and already the burdens of a man on his t'in little shoulders. Your poor father hasn't slept a full night since this happened. Did you know that? He had such high hopes for Billy. He wanted you both to go to college and not have to work as hard as he's had to all his life. And now look. You have more sense than that, Ben. Don't let life trap you.

BILL enters. He has changed his pants and is buttoning a clean white shirt. MARY goes into the dining room and begins to remove the tablecloth from the dining room table.

BILL

Mom, what about Dad? He won't start picking on the priest, will he? You know how he likes to argue.

MARY

He won't say a word, my son. You needn't worry. Worry more about Minnie showing up.

BILL

What if he's drunk?

MARY

He won't be. Your father knows better than to sound off in church. Oh, and another t'ing—he wants you to polish his shoes for tonight. They're in the bedroom. The polish is on your dresser. You needn't be too fussy.

BEN

I'll do his shoes, Mom. Billy's all dressed.

MARY

No, no, Ben, that's all right. He asked Billy to.

BILL

What did Ben do this time?

MARY

He didn't do anyt'ing.

BILL

He must have.

MARY

Is it too much trouble to polish your father's shoes, after all he does for you? If you won't do it, I'll do it myself.

BILL

(indignantly) How come when Dad's mad at Ben, I get all the dirty jobs? Jeez! Will I be glad to get out of here! *(Rolling up his shirt sleeves he exits into his bedroom.)*

MARY takes a clean white linen tablecloth from a drawer in the cabinet and covers the table. During the following scene she sets five places with her good glasses, silverware and plates.

BEN

(slight pause) Billy's right, isn't he? What'd I do, Mom?

MARY

Take it up with your father. I'm tired of being the middle man.

BEN

Is it because of last night? *(slight pause)* It is, isn't it?

MARY

He t'inks you didn't want him there, Ben. He t'inks you're ashamed of him.

BEN

He wouldn't have gone, Mom. That's the only reason I never invited him.

MARY

He would have went, last night.

BEN

(angrily) He's never even been to one lousy Parents' Night in thirteen years. Not one! And he calls **me** contrary!

MARY

You listen to me. Your father never got past Grade T'ree. He was yanked out of school and made to work. In those days, back home, he was lucky to get that much and don't kid yourself.

BEN

Yeah? So?

MARY

So? So he's afraid to. He's afraid of sticking out. Is that so hard to understand? Is it?

BEN

What're you getting angry about? All I said was—

MARY

You say he don't take an interest, but he was proud enough to show off your report cards all those years. I suppose with you that don't count for much.

BEN

All right. But he never goes anywhere without you, Mom, and last night you were here at the shower.

MARY

Last night was different, Ben, and you ought to know that. It was your high school graduation. He would have went with me or without me. If you'd only asked him.

A truck horn blasts twice.

There he is now in the driveway. Whatever happens, don't fall for his old tricks. He'll be looking for a fight, and doing his best to find any excuse. *(calling)* Billy, you hear that? Don't complain about the shoes, once your father comes!

BEN

(urgently) Mom, there's something I want to tell you before Dad comes in.

MARY

Sure, my son. Go ahead. I'm listening. What's on your mind?

BEN

Well . . .

MARY

(smiling) Come on. It can't be that bad.

BEN

(slight pause) I want to move out, Mom.

MARY

(almost inaudibly) . . . What?

BEN

I said I want to move out.

MARY

(softly, as she sets the cutlery) I heard you. *(pause)* What for?

BEN

I just think it's time. I'll be nineteen soon. *(pause)* I'm moving in with Billy and Kathy and help pay the rent. *(pause)* I won't be far away. I'll see you on weekends. *(MARY nods.)* Mom?

MARY

(absently) What?

BEN

Will you tell Dad? *(slight pause)* Mom? Did you hear me?

MARY

I heard you. He'll be upset, I can tell you. By rights you ought to tell him yourself.

BEN

If I do, we'll just get in a big fight and you know it. He'll take it better, coming from you.

The front door opens and JACOB MERCER enters whistling 'I's the b'y'. He is fifty, though he looks older. He is dressed in a peaked cap, carpenter's overalls, thick-soled workboots, and a lumberjack shirt over a T-shirt. Under one arm he carries his black lunchpail.

MARY
Your suit! I knowed it!

JACOB
Don't get in an uproar, now. I left it sitting on the front seat of the truck. *(He looks at BEN, then back to MARY.)* Is Billy home?

MARY
He's in the bedroom, polishing your shoes.

JACOB
(Crosses to the bedroom door.) Billy, my son, come out a moment.

BILL enters, carrying a shoe brush.

Put down the brush and go out in my truck and bring me back the tux on the seat.

BILL
What's wrong with Ben? He's not doing anything.

JACOB
Don't ask questions. That's a good boy. I'd ask your brother, but he always has a good excuse.

BEN
I'll go get it. *(He starts for the front door.)*

JACOB
(calling after BEN) Oh, it's too late to make up now. The damage is done.

MARY
Don't talk nonsense, Jacob.

JACOB

(*a last thrust*) And aside from that—I wouldn't want you dirtying your nice clean hands in your father's dirty old truck!

The front door closes on his last words. BILL returns to his room. JACOB sets his lunchpail and his cap on the dining room table.

JACOB

Did he get his diploma?

MARY

Yes. It's in the bedroom.

JACOB

(*Breaks into a smile and lifts his cap.*) And will you gaze on Mary over there. When I stepped in the door, I t'ought the Queen had dropped in for tea.

MARY

You didn't even notice.

JACOB

Come here, my dear, and give Jacob a kiss.

MARY

(*She darts behind the table, laughing.*) I'll give Jacob a swift boot in the rear end with my pointed toe.

JACOB grabs her, rubs his rough cheek against hers.

You'll take the skin off! Jake! You're far too rough! And watch my new dress! Don't rip it.

JACOB releases her and breaks into a little jig as he sings.

> I's the b'y that builds the boat
> And I's the b'y that sails her,
> I's the b'y that catches the fish
> And takes 'em home to Lizer.

Sods and rinds to cover your flake
Cake and tea for supper
Codfish in the spring of the year
Fried in maggoty butter.

I don't want your maggoty fish
Cake and tea for winter
I could buy as good as that
Down in Bona Vista.

I took Lizer to a dance
And faith but she could travel
And every step that she did take
Was up to her ass in gravel.

JACOB ends the song with a little step or flourish.

MARY
There's no mistakin' where you've been to, and it's not to church.

JACOB
All right, now, I had one little glass, and don't you start.

MARY
(as she re-enters the kitchen) How many?

JACOB
I can't lie, Mary. *(He puts his hand on his heart.)* As God is my witness—two. Two glasses to celebrate the wedding of my youngest son. *(He follows her into the kitchen.)*

MARY
Half a dozen's more like it, unless you expects God to perjure himself for the likes of you. Well, no odds: you're just in time. Kathy'll soon be here, so get cleaned up.

JACOB
I washed up on the job.

MARY

Well, change your old clothes. You're not sitting down with the likes of that on. *(She returns to the dining room with bread and butter for the dining room table.)*

JACOB

I suppose it's fish with Kathy coming and him now a bloody Mick. Next t'ing you knows he'll be expecting me to chant grace in Latin.

MARY

And I'll crown you if you opens your yap like that around Kathy. Don't you dare.

JACOB

(Following MARY, he sits at the dining room table.) 'Course we could have the priest drop by and bless the table himself. *(He makes the sign of the cross.)*

MARY

Jacob!

JACOB

Though I doubts he could get his Cadillac in the driveway.

MARY

(back to kitchen) If you comes out with the likes of that tonight, I'll never speak to you again. You hear?

JACOB

Ah, go on with you. What do you know? If you had nothing in your pockets but holes, a priest wouldn't give you t'read to sew it with.

BEN

(Enters with the box.) I put your toolbox down in the basement while I was at it, Dad. And rolled up the windows in your truck, in case it rains tonight.

JACOB

Did you, now? And I'm supposed to forget all about last night, is that it? Pretend it never occurred? Your brother's good enough for you but not your own father. *(as BEN crosses to kitchen)* Well, it would take more than that to stitch up the hurt, I can assure you. And a long time before it heals. Don't be looking to your mother for support.

BEN

I wasn't. *(He sits at kitchen table.)*

JACOB

Or for sympathy, either.

MARY

Jacob, it don't serve no purpose to look for a fight.

JACOB

(to MARY) You keep your two cents worth out of it. Nobody asked you. You got too much to say.

Enter BILL, carrying the shined shoes, which he gives to his father.

BILL

Hey, Dad, do me a favour? When Kathy gets here, no cracks about the Pope's nose and stuff like that. And just for once don't do that Squid-Jiggin' thing and take your teeth out. Okay? *(He sits at table across from his father and reads the evening paper.)*

JACOB

Well, listen to him, now. *(to MARY)* Who put him up to that? You? Imagine. Telling me what I can say and do in my own house.

MARY

(returning to dining room) Billy, my son, I got a feeling you just walked into it. *(She takes a polishing cloth from cabinet and rubs her good silverware, including a large fish-knife.)*

JACOB

(to BILL) If you only knowed what my poor father went t'rough with the Catholics. Oh, if you only knowed, you wouldn't be doing this. My own son a turncoat. And back home, when we was growing up, you wouldn't dare go where the Catholics lived after dark. You'd be murdered, and many's the poor boy was. Knocked over the head and drownded, and all they done was let night catch them on a Catholic road. My father's brother was one. Poor Isaac. He was just fifteen, that summer. Tied with his arms behind him and tossed in the pond like a stone. My poor father never forgot that to his dying day.

The family wait out the harangue.

And here you is j'ining their ranks! T'ree weeks of instructions. By the jumping Jesus Christ you don't come from my side of the family. I'm glad my poor father never lived to see this day, I can tell you. The loyalest Orangeman that ever marched in a church parade, my father. He'd turn over in his grave if he saw a grandson of his kissing the Pope's ass. Promising to bring up your poor innocent babies Roman Catholics and them as ignorant of Rome as earthworms.

      Oh, it's a good t'ing for you, my son, that he ain't around to see it, because sure as you'm there he'd march into that church tomorrow with his belt in his hand, and take that smirk off your face! Billy, my son, I never expected this of you, of all people. No, I didn't. Not you. If it was your brother, now, I could understand it. He'd do it just for spite. . . .

MARY

Hold your tongue, boy. Don't you ever run down? I just hope to goodness Ben don't call on you at the wedding to toast the bride and groom. We'll all be old before it's over. *(slight pause)* Did you try on your tux?

JACOB

No, boy, it was too crowded.

MARY

Then try it on. You're worse than the kids. *(She hands him the box.)* Go on.

JACOB

(to BILL, referring to the shoes) T'anks. *(He exits into his bedroom.)*

MARY

Ben, do your mother a favour? Fill up the glasses. I left the jug in the kitchen. *(She sits at the dining room table, checks and folds five linen napkins.)* Look at him, Ben. The little fart. My baby. *(to herself)* How quick it all goes. . . . I can still see us to this day . . . the t'ree of us . . . coming up from Newfoundland . . . July of 1945 . . . the war not yet over. . . . Father gone ahead to look for work on construction . . . that old train packed with soldiers, and do you t'ink a single one would rise off his big fat backside to offer up his seat? Not on your life. There we was, huddled together out on the brakes, a couple, t'ree hours . . . with the wind and the soot from the engine blowing back . . . until a lady come out and saw us. 'Well, the likes of this I've never seen,' she says. 'I've got four sons in the war, and if one of mine was in that carriage, I'd disown 'im!'

We've never had anyt'ing to be ashamed of, my sons. We've been poor . . . but we've always stuck together. *(to BILL)* Is you frightened, my son?

BILL

No. Why should I be?

MARY

Don't be ashamed of it. Tomorrow you'll most likely wish you was back with your mother and father in your own soft bed.

BEN

He's scared shitless, Mom. *(to BILL)* Tell the truth.

MARY

Ben, is that nice talk?

BILL

(*to BEN*) I'll trade places.

MARY

Well, as long as you loves her, that's all that matters. Without that there's nothing, and with it what you don't have can wait. But a word of warning, Billy—don't come running to us with your squabbles, because we won't stick our noses into it. And before I forgets—you'd better not say a word to your father about Ben moving out. I'll tell him myself after the wedding.

JACOB

(*off*) Mary!

MARY

(*calling*) What is it, boy?

JACOB

(*off*) Come here! I can't get this goddamn button fast!

MARY

(*shaking her head*) It's one of those mysteries how he made it t'rough life this far. If he didn't have me, he wouldn't know which leg of his pants was which. (*She exits.*)

BILL

(*slight pause*) You told her, huh? She doesn't seem to mind.

BEN

Keep your voice down. You want Dad to hear?

BILL

What did she say? Is she going to tell him?

BEN

Yeah, but do you think I ought to let her?

BILL

What do you mean?

BEN

Well, maybe I should tell him myself.

BILL

Are you crazy?

BEN

If I don't, you know what'll happen. Mom'll get all the shit.

BILL

(*pause*) Ben, you really want to do this? Are you sure?

BEN

Look—my books and tuition're paid for. All I got to worry about is the rent. I can handle that, waiting on tables. I'll make out. Listen, whose idea was it anyhow? Mine or yours? I wouldn't do it if I didn't want to.

BILL

Okay.

BEN

I need to, Billy. Christ, you know that. Either Dad goes, or I do.

BILL

I wish I felt that way. I don't want to move out. I don't want to get married. I don't know the first thing about girls. I mean, Kathy's the first girl I ever did it with. No kidding. The very first. We've only done it four or five times. The first time was in a cemetery, for Chrissake!

BEN

Well, at least you've been laid, Billy. I never.

BILL

Really? (*he laughs—pause*) I like Kathy. I like her a lot. But I don't know what else. What do you think Dad would do, if he was in my shoes? I think if Kathy was Mom he'd marry her, don't you?

MARY

(*Enters.*) Listen to me, you two. I don't want either one of you to say one word or snicker even when your father comes out. Is that understood?

BEN

What's wrong?

MARY

They give him the wrong coat. I suppose he was in such a rush to get to the Oakwood he didn't bother trying it on.

Enter JACOB singing, now dressed in the rental tux and polished shoes. The sleeves are miles too short for him, the back hiked up. He looks like a caricature of discomfort.

Here comes the bride,
All fat and wide,
See how she wobbles
From side to side.

The boys glance at one another and try to keep from breaking up.

JACOB

Well, boys, am I a fit match for your mother?

BEN

Dad, I wish I had a camera.

JACOB

Is you making fun?

MARY

No, he's not. The sleeves are a sight, but—(*giving BEN a censorious look*)—aside from that it's a perfect fit. Couldn't be better. Could it, Billy?

BILL

Made to measure, Dad.

JACOB

I t'ink I'll kick up my heels. I'm right in the mood. *(as he crosses to the record player)* What do you say, Mary? Feel up to it? *(He selects a record.)*

MARY

I'm willing, if you is, Jake.

JACOB

All right, boys, give us room. *(The record starts to play—a rousing tune with lots of fiddles.)* Your mother loves to twirl her skirt and show off her drawers! *(He seizes his wife, and they whirl around the room, twirling and stomping with enjoyment and abandon.)*

BEN

Go, Mom! *(He whistles.)*

BILL and BEN clap their hands to the music.

Give her hell, Dad!

MARY

Not so fast, Jacob, you'll make me dizzy!

JACOB stops after a few turns. He is slightly dizzy. He sits.

JACOB

(to BILL) Dance with your mother. I galled my heel at work. *(BILL does.)* You ought to have seen your mother in her day, Ben. She'd turn the head of a statue. There wasn't a man from Bareneed to Bay Roberts didn't blink when she passed by.

MARY

Come on, Ben. Before it's over. *(She takes BEN, and they dance around the room.)*

JACOB

That's one t'ing about Ben, Mary. He won't ever leave you. The day he gets married himself he'll move in next door.

Finally MARY collapses laughing on the chesterfield. The music plays on.

JACOB

(expansively) I t'ink a drink's in order. What do you say, boys? To whet the appetite. *(He searches in the bottom of the cabinet. To MARY)* Where's all the whiskey to? You didn't t'row it out, did you?

MARY

You t'rowed it down your t'roat, that's where it was t'rowed.

JACOB

Well, boys, looks like there's no whiskey. *(He holds up a bottle.)* How does a little 'screech' sound?

BEN

Not for me, Dad.

JACOB

Why not?

BEN

I just don't like it.

JACOB

(sarcastically) No, you wouldn't. I suppose it's too strong for you. Well, Billy'll have some, won't you, my son? *(He turns down the music.)*

BILL

(surprised) I will?

JACOB

Get two glasses out, then, and let's have a quick drink. *(BILL does and hands a glass to his father.)* Don't suppose you'd have a little drop, Mary, my love? *(He winks at BILL.)*

MARY

Go on with you. You ought to have better sense, teaching the boys all your bad habits. And after you promised your poor mother on her death-bed you'd warn them off alcohol . . .

JACOB

Don't talk foolishness. A drop of this won't harm a soul. Might even do some good, all you know.

MARY

Yes, some good it's done you.

JACOB

At least I'd take a drink with my own father, if he was alive. I'd do that much, my lady.

MARY

(quickly) Pay no attention, Ben. (to JACOB) And listen, I don't want you getting tight and making a disgrace of yourself at the rehearsal tonight. You hear?

JACOB

Oh, I'll be just as sober as the priest, rest assured of that. And you just study his fingers, if they'm not as brown as a new potato from nicotine. I dare say if he didn't swallow Sen-Sen, you'd know where all that communion wine goes to. (to BILL) How many drunks you suppose is wearing Roman collars? More than the Pope would dare admit. And all those t'ousands of babies they keep digging up in the basements of convents. It's shocking.

BEN

That's a lot of bull, Dad.

JACOB

It is, is it? Who told you that? Is that more of the stuff you learns at university? Your trouble is you've been brainwashed.

BEN

You just want to believe all that.

MARY

And you'd better not come out with that tonight, if you knows what's good for you.

JACOB

(to BILL) Mind—I'm giving you fair warning. I won't sprinkle my face with holy water or make the sign of the cross. And nothing in this world or the next can persuade me.

BILL

You don't have to, Dad. Relax.

JACOB

Just so you knows.

BEN

All you got to do, Dad, is sit there in the front row and look sweet.

JACOB

All right, there's no need to get saucy. I wasn't talking to you! *(He pours a little 'screech' in the two glasses. To BILL)* Here's to you, boy. You got the makings of a man. That's more than I can say for your older brother.

JACOB downs his drink. BILL glances helplessly at BEN. He doesn't drink.

Go on.

BILL hesitates, then downs it, grimacing and coughing.

You see that, Mary? *(his anger rising)* It's your fault the other one's the way he is. It's high time, my lady, you let go and weaned him away from the tit!

MARY

(angrily) You shut your mouth. There's no call for that kind of talk!

JACOB

He needs more in his veins than mother's milk, goddamn it!

BEN

(shouting at JACOB) What're you screaming at her for? She didn't do anything!

JACOB

(a semblance of sudden calm) Well, listen to him, now. Look at the murder in his face. One harsh word to his mother and up comes his fists. I'll bet you wouldn't be half so quick to defend your father.

MARY

Be still, Jacob. You don't know what you're saying.

JACOB

He t'inks he's too good to drink with me!

BEN

All right, I will, if it's that important. Only let's not fight.

MARY

He's just taunting you into it, Ben. Don't let him.

JACOB

(sarcastically) No, my son, your mother's right. I wouldn't wish for your downfall on my account. To hear her tell it I'm the devil tempting Saul on the road to Damascus.

MARY

Well, the devil better learn his scripture, if he wants to quote it. The devil tempted our Lord in the wilderness, and Saul had a revelation on the road to Damascus.

JACOB

A revelation! *(He turns off the record.)* I'll give you a revelation!
I'm just a piece of shit around here! Who is it wears himself
out year after year to give him a roof over his head and food
in his mouth? Who buys his clothes and keeps him in university?

MARY

He buys his own clothes, and he's got a scholarship.

JACOB

(furious) Oh, butt out! You'd stick up for him if it meant your
life, and never once put in a good word for me.

MARY

I'm only giving credit where credit's due.

JACOB

Liar.

MARY

Ah, go on. You're a fine one to talk. You'd call the ace of spades
white and not bat an eye.

JACOB

(enraged) It never fails. I can't get my own son to do the simplest
goddamn t'ing without a row. No matter what.

BEN

It's never simple, Dad. You never let it be simple or I might.
It's always a **test**.

JACOB

Test!

MARY

Ben, don't get drawn into it.

JACOB

(to BEN) The sooner you learns to get along with others, the
sooner you'll grow up. Test!

BEN

Do you ever hear yourself? 'Ben, get up that ladder. You want
people to think you're a sissy?' 'Have a drink, Ben. It'll make
a man out of you!'

JACOB

I said no such t'ing, now. Liar.

BEN

It's what you **meant**. 'Cut your hair, Ben. You look like a girl.'
The same shit over and over, and it never stops!

JACOB

Now it all comes out. You listening to this, Mary?

BEN

No, you listen, Dad. You don't really expect me to climb that
ladder or take that drink. You want me to refuse, don't you?

JACOB

Well, listen to him. The faster you gets out into the real world
the better for you. *(He turns away.)*

BEN

Dad, you don't want me to be a man, you just want to impress
me with how much less of a man I am than you. *(He snatches
the bottle from his father and takes a swig.)* All right. Look. *(He
rips open his shirt.)* I still haven't got hair on my chest, and I'm
still not a threat to you.

JACOB

No, and you'm not likely ever to be, either, until you grows
up and gets out from under your mother's skirts.

BEN

No, Dad—until I get out from under **yours**.

The doorbell rings.

MARY

That's Kathy. All right, that's more than enough for one night. Let's have no more bickering. Jake, get dressed. And not another word out of anyone. The poor girl will t'ink she's fallen in with a pack of wild savages.

JACOB

(getting in the last word) And there's no bloody mistakin' who the wild savage is. *(With that he exits into his bedroom.)*

MARY

Billy, answer the door. *(to BEN)* And you—change your shirt. You look a fright.

BEN exits. BILL opens the front door, and KATHY enters. She is sixteen, very pretty, but at the moment her face is pale and emotionless.

KATHY

Hello, Mrs. Mercer.

MARY

You're just in time, Kathy. *(MARY gives her a kiss.)* Take her coat, Billy. I'll be right out, dear. *(She exits.)*

KATHY

Where is everyone?

BILL

(taking her coat) Getting dressed. *(As he tries to kiss her, she pulls away her cheek.)*

BILL

What's wrong? *(He hangs up her coat.)*

KATHY

Nothing. I don't feel well.

BILL

Why not? Did you drink too much at the party?

KATHY

What party?

BILL

Didn't the girls at work throw a party for you this afternoon?

KATHY

I didn't go to the office this afternoon.

BILL

You didn't go? What do you mean?

KATHY

Just what I said.

BILL

What **did** you say?

KATHY

Will you get off my back!

BILL

What did I say? *(slight pause)* Are you mad at me?

KATHY

(Looks at him.) Billy, do you love me? Do you? I need to know.

BILL

What's happened, Kathy?

KATHY

I'm asking you a simple question.

BILL

And I want to know what's happened.

KATHY

If I hadn't been pregnant, you'd never have wanted to get married, would you?

BILL

So?

KATHY

I hate you.

BILL

For Chrissake, Kathy, what's happened?

KATHY

(Sits on the chesterfield.) I lost the baby. . . .

BILL

What?

KATHY

Isn't that good news?

BILL

What the hell happened?

KATHY

I started bleeding in the ladies' room this morning.

BILL

Bleeding? What do you mean?

KATHY

Haemorrhaging. I screamed, and one of the girls rushed me to the hospital. I think the people at work thought I'd done something to myself.

BILL

Had you?

KATHY

Of course not. You know I wouldn't.

BILL

What did the doctor say?

KATHY

I had a miscarriage. *(She looks up at him.)* You're not even sorry, are you?

BILL

I am, really. What else did the doctor say?

KATHY

I lost a lot of blood. I'm supposed to eat lots of liver and milk, to build it up. You should have seen me, Billy. I was white and shaky. I'm a little better now. I've been sleeping all afternoon.

BILL

(slight pause) What was it?

KATHY

What was what?

BILL

The baby.

KATHY

Do you really want to know?

BILL doesn't answer.

BILL

What'll we do?

KATHY

Tell our folks, I guess. My mother doesn't know yet. She's been at the track all day with her boyfriend. *(slight pause)* I haven't told anyone else, Billy. Just you.

Enter JACOB and MARY. He is dressed in a pair of slacks and a white shirt. He carries a necktie in his hand. MARY wears a blouse and skirt.

JACOB

Billy, my son, tie me a Windsor knot. That's a good boy. *(He hands BILL the necktie and BILL proceeds to make the knot. Shyly, to KATHY)* Hello, my dear. *(KATHY nods.)* Lovely old day.

MARY

Come on. We may as well sit right down before it colds off.

I'll serve up the fish and potatoes. *(She transfers the fish and potatoes into serving dishes.)*

JACOB
(calling) Ben! *(to KATHY, referring to the tie)* I'm all t'umbs or I'd do it myself.

BEN
(Enters, his shirt changed.) Hi, Kathy.

KATHY
Hi, Ben. Congratulations.

BEN
For what?

KATHY
Didn't you graduate last night?

BEN
Oh. Yeah.

JACOB
I suppose if Ben ever becomes Prime Minister, I'll be the last to know unless I reads it in the newspapers.

MARY
Kathy, you sit right down there, dear. Billy, you sit next to her. And Ben's right here.

BILL hands his father the tie. JACOB slips it on as he approaches the table.

Father, why don't you say grace?

JACOB
Maybe Kathy would like to.

KATHY
We never say grace at our house.

JACOB

Is that a fact? Imagine.

BILL

(*jumping in*) 'Bless this food that now we take, and feed our souls for Jesus' sake. Amen.'

ALL

Amen. (*They dig in.*)

JACOB

Have an eye to the bones, Kathy. (*slight pause*) You was born in Toronto, wasn't you? Someday you'll have to take a trip home, you and Billy, and see how they dries the cod on the beaches. He don't remember any more than you. He was just little when he come up here.

MARY

That was a long time ago, Kathy. 1945.

KATHY

(*slight pause*) Have you been home since, Mr. Mercer?

JACOB

No, my dear, and I don't know if I wants to. A different generation growing up now. (*glancing at BEN*) A different brand of Newfie altogether. And once the oldtimers die off, that'll be the end of it. Newfoundland'll never be the same after that, I can tell you. (*slight pause*) Do you know what flakes is?

KATHY

No.

JACOB

Well, they'm spread over the shore—these wooden stages they dries the codfish on. Sometimes—and this is no word of a lie, is it, Mary?—the fishflies'll buzz around that codfish as t'ick as the hairs on your arm. (*slight pause*) T'icker. T'ick as tarpaper.

MARY

Jacob, we're eating. *(to KATHY)* He's just like his poor mother, Jacob is. She'd start on about the tapeworm as you was lifting the pork to your mouth. *(to JACOB)* Let the poor girl eat in peace, Father. *(to KATHY)* You've hardly touched your food, dear. Has he spoiled your appetite? It wouldn't be the first time.

KATHY

I'm just not too hungry, Mrs. Mercer.

MARY

I understands. Big day tomorrow. I was the same way, my wedding day. It's a wonder I didn't faint.

JACOB

(slight pause–to KATHY) You notice Ben don't look my way? He's sore.

KATHY glances at BEN, who goes on eating, oblivious.

JACOB

(to KATHY) Oh, he knows how to dish it out with the best, but he can't take it. You can joke with Billy, he likes a bit of fun, but with the other one you don't dare open your mouth.

BEN

Will you shut up, Dad?

JACOB

(to KATHY) I'll bet you didn't get sore with your poor father and talk back all the time when he was alive, did you, my dear? No, that's what you didn't. You had more respect. And I bet now you don't regret it.

MARY

Don't ask the child to choose sides, Jacob. You've got no right to do that. Anyhow, Kathy's got more sense than to get mixed up in it. Don't you, Kathy?

JACOB

The Bible says to honour thy father and thy mother. . . .

MARY

(exasperated) Oh, hold your tongue, for goodness sake. Don't your jaw ever get tired?

JACOB

(to KATHY) Well, you can see for yourself what happens, my dear. Anyone in this room is free to say what they likes about the old man, but just let him criticize back and you'd t'ink a fox had burst into the chicken coop, the way Mother Mercer here gathers her first-born under her wing. *(slight pause–to KATHY, but meant for his wife)* I suppose by now you've heard your mother and me once went together? I suppose Minnie's mentioned it often enough? Fine figure of a woman, Minnie. Still looks as good as ever.

BILL

I hear you used to be a real woman's man, Dad.

JACOB

Who told you that?

BILL

Mom.

MARY

(quickly) Liar. I told you no such t'ing.

BILL

You did so. Didn't she, Ben?

BEN smiles at his mother.

JACOB

Well, contrary to what your mother tells, that particular year I had only one sweetheart, and that was Minnie Jackson. Wasn't it, Mary?

MARY

(*nodding*) She was still a Fraser then. That was the same year I was going with Jerome McKenzie. Wasn't it, Jacob?

JACOB

Oh, don't forget the most important part, Mary, the Q.C., the Queen's Counsel. Jerome McKenzie, Q.C. (*to KATHY*) Jerome's a well-known barrister in St. John's, and Mrs. Mercer's all the time t'rowing him up in my face. Ain't you, Mary? Never lets me forget it, will you? (*to KATHY*) You see, my dear, she might have married Jerome McKenzie, Q.C., and never had a single worry in the world, if it wasn't for me. Ain't that so, Mary?

MARY

If you insists, Jacob.

BILL and KATHY stare silently at their plates, embarrassed. BEN looks from his father to his mother and then to BILL.

BEN

Did you get the boutonnieres and cuff links for the ushers?

MARY

It's all taken care of, my son. (*pause*) What kind of flowers did your mother order, Kathy?

KATHY

Red roses.

MARY

How nice.

KATHY

I like yellow roses better, but—(*She stops abruptly.*)

BILL

But what?

KATHY

Nothing.

MARY

Yellow roses mean tears, my son.

KATHY

Did you carry roses, Mrs. Mercer?

MARY

I did. Red butterfly roses. And I wore a gown of white satin, with a lace veil. I even had a crown of orange blossoms.

KATHY

I'll bet you were beautiful.

JACOB

My dear, she lit up that little Anglican church like the Second Coming. I suppose I told you all about the wedding ring?

MARY

No, you didn't, and she don't want to hear tell of it, and neither do the rest of us. Don't listen to his big fibs, Kathy.

JACOB

I still remembers that day. I had on my gaberdine suit, with a white carnation in the lapel. In those days Mary t'ought I was handsome.

MARY

Get to the point, Father.

JACOB

We was that poor I couldn't afford a ring, so when the Reverend Mr. Price got t'rough with the dearly beloveds and asked for the ring, I reached into my pocket and give him all I had—an old bent nail.

MARY

Last time it was a cigar band.

JACOB

(still to KATHY) And if you was to ask me today, twenty years

later, if it's been worth it—my dear, my answer would still be the same, for all her many faults—that old rusty nail has brung me more joy and happiness than you can ever imagine. And I wouldn't trade the old woman here, nor a blessed hair of her head, not for all the gold bullion in the Vatican.

BILL

Dad.

JACOB

And my name's not Jerome McKenzie, Q.C., either. And the likes of Ben here may t'ink me just an old fool, not worth a second t'ought—

BEN *shoves back his plate, holding back his temper.*

—and run me down to my face the first chance he gets—

BEN

Ah, shut up.

JACOB

—and treat me with no more respect and consideration than you would your own worst enemy!—

BEN

Will you grow up! (*He knocks over his chair and exits into his bedroom.*)

JACOB

(*shouting after him*)—but I've always done what I seen fit, and no man can do more! (*The door slams—slight pause.*) I won't say another word.

MARY

You've said enough, brother. (*slight pause*) What Kathy must t'ink of us! (*slight pause*) And then you wonders why he's the way he is, when you sits there brazen-faced and makes him feel like two cents in front of company. You haven't a grain of sense, you haven't!

JACOB

Did I say a word of a lie? Did I?

MARY

No, you always speaks the gospel truth, you do.

JACOB

I never could say two words in a row to that one, without he takes offence. Not two bloody words!

MARY collects the supper plates. BILL and KATHY remain seated.

Look. He didn't finish half his plate. *(calling)* Come out and eat the rest of your supper, Ben. There's no food wasted in this house. *(slight pause)* Take it in to him, Mary.

MARY

(picking up BEN's chair) You—you're the cause of it. You're enough to spoil anyone's appetite.

JACOB

Ah, for Christ's sake, he's too damn soft, and you don't help any. I was out fishing on the Labrador when I was ten years old, six months of the year for ten dollars, and out of that ten dollars had to come my rubber boots. *(to KATHY)* Ten years old, and I had to stand up and take it like a man. *(to MARY)* That's a lot tougher than a few harsh words from his father!

MARY

(as she serves the dessert) And you'll make him hard, is that it, Jacob? Hard and tough like yourself? Blame him for all you've suffered. Make him pay for all you never had.

JACOB

Oh, shut up, Mary, you don't understand these matters. He won't have you or me to fall back on once he gets out into the world. He'll need to be strong or—*(He winks at BILL.)*—he'll end up like your cousin Israel.

MARY

And don't tell **that** story, Jacob. You're at the table.

JACOB

(to KATHY) Israel Parsons was Mrs. Mercer's first cousin.

MARY

Might as well talk to a log.

JACOB

He was a law student at the time, and he worked summers at the pulp and paper mill at Corner Brook, cleaning the machines. Well, one noon hour he crawled inside a machine to clean the big sharp blades, and someone flicked on the switch. Poor young Israel was ground up into pulp. They didn't find a trace of him, did they, Mary? Not even a hair. Mary's poor mother always joked that he was the only one of her relatives ever to make the headlines—if you knows what I mean.

MARY

She knows. And just what has Israel Parsons got to do with Ben, pray tell?

JACOB

Because that's what the world will do to Ben, Mary, if he's not strong. Chew him up alive and swallow him down without a trace. Mark my words. *(He lifts the bowl to his mouth and drinks the peach juice.)*

The front door bursts open.

MINNIE

(off) Anybody home?

JACOB

Minnie! *(He glances at MARY, then rises.)*

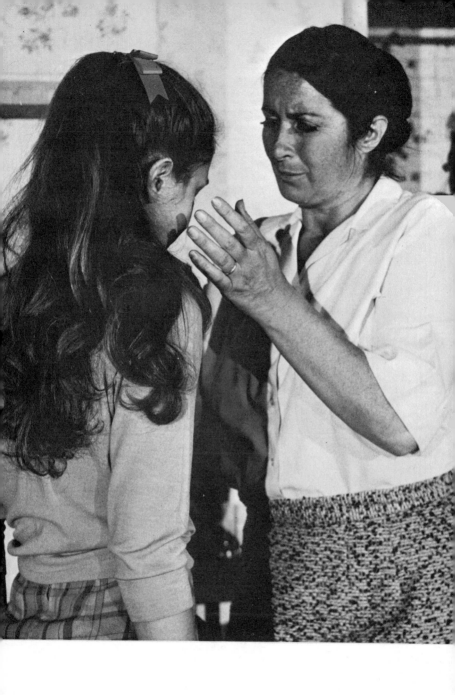

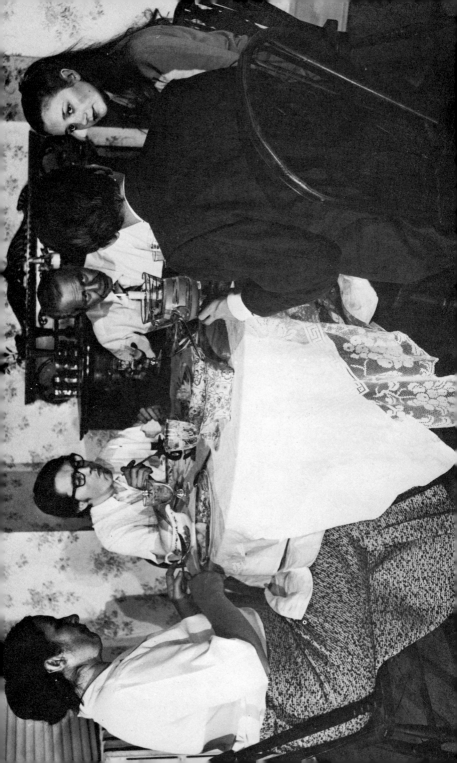

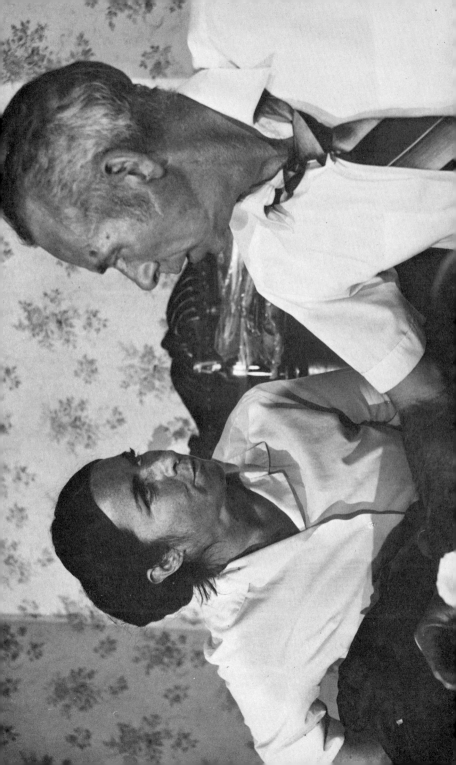

MINNIE enters. She is in her late forties, boisterous and voluptuous, a little flashily dressed.

MINNIE

Is you still eating?

JACOB

No, come in, come in.

MINNIE

If you is—guess what?—I brung along me new boyfriend to spoil your appetites. . . . Where's he to? Can't keep track of the bugger! *(She returns to the hallway, and shouts offstage.)* For Christ's sake, you dirty t'ing, you! You might have waited till you got inside!

KATHY

(to BILL) What's **she** doing here?

MINNIE

(off) Come on. There's no need to be shy.

HAROLD enters with MINNIE. He is conservatively dressed but sports a white carnation.

MINNIE

(to HAROLD) That's Jacob and Mary. This here's Harold. *(They shake hands.)*

JACOB

Here, give me your coats. *(He takes the coats.)*

MINNIE

T'anks, boy. *(to KATHY)* Hello, sister! Still mad at me?

KATHY doesn't answer.

MINNIE

(to MARY) Harold works in a funeral parlour. He's an embalmer. Imagine. We met when poor Willard died. He worked on his corpse.

MARY

(*incredulously*) You made that up, Minnie. Confess.

MINNIE

As God is me witness, maid!

JACOB

Just so long as you'm not drumming up business, Harold.

HAROLD doesn't crack a smile.

MINNIE

He ain't got an ounce of humour in his body, Harold. (*looking at JACOB*) But he's got two or t'ree pounds of what counts. Don't you, Lazarus?

KATHY

(*sharply*) Mother!

MINNIE

'Mother' yourself. (*sitting on arm of chesterfield next to HAROLD*) I calls him Lazarus because he comes to life at night. And what a resurrection. Ah, I'm so wicked, Mary. To tell you the truth, I haven't been exactly mourning since Willard died, as sister over there can testify. And I'll tell you why. I took a good solid look at Willard—God rest his soul!—stretched out in his casket the t'ree days of his wake, all powdered and rouged and made up like a total stranger, and I says to myself, Minnie, live it up, maid. This is all there is, this life. You're dead a good long time. (*to JACOB*) And I for one wouldn't bet a t'in dime on the hereafter, and God knows I've t'rowed hundreds of dollars away on long shots in my day.

JACOB

Now, Minnie, enough of the religion. Would you both care for a whiskey? (*MARY reacts.*)

MINNIE

(*meaning HAROLD*) Look at his ears pick up. Sure, Jake. That's one of the reasons we come early.

JACOB crosses to the cabinet during MINNIE's speech and brings out a bottle of whiskey. He pours three drinks.

And Mary, I got to apologize for last night. I suppose I'll never live it down. I don't know what happened, maid. I laid down with a drink in me hand after supper and the next t'ing I know it's this morning and I'm in the doghouse.

MARY
That's okay, Minnie. *(She sits.)*

JACOB
Billy, my son, bring me the ginger ale. That's a good boy.

During the dialogue BILL fetches the ginger ale from the fridge and returns to the dining room table.

How do you like your drink, Minnie?

MINNIE
A little mix in mine, and not'ing in Harold's. The ginger ale tickles his nose and gets him all excited.

JACOB
What is he, Minnie? Newfie?

MINNIE
No, boy—Canadian.

JACOB
Harold, there's only two kinds of people in this world—Newfies and them that wishes they was.

MINNIE
That's what I tells him, boy.

JACOB
Why else would Canada have j'ined us in '49? Right, Minnie? *(JACOB crosses to chesterfield with the drinks.)*

MARY

I t'ought you didn't have no whiskey? I t'ought all you had in the house was 'screech'? Do you mean to tell me that was deliberate, what you put Ben t'rough?

JACOB

(quickly changing the subject) Minnie, don't you want to see the shower gifts?

MINNIE

Sure, boy. Where's they to?

JACOB

They're in the bedroom. Show her, Mary. Now's a good time.

MARY rises and crosses to the bedroom door. MINNIE follows.

MINNIE

(indicating HAROLD) Don't give him any more to drink, Jacob, till I gets back. The bugger likes to get a head start.

They exit.

MINNIE

(off) Maid, will you look! A gift shop! Jesus!

JACOB

(slight pause—to HAROLD, embarrassed) Well.

HAROLD nods. They drink.

MINNIE

(off) Even a rolling pin! *(She pokes out her head.)* My Jesus, Harold, I finally found somet'ing that compares!

JACOB glances at HAROLD. HAROLD glances at JACOB. They drink.

JACOB

(after a moment) Grand old day.

HAROLD nods. Silence.

JACOB
(after a moment) Couldn't ask for better.

HAROLD nods. Silence.

JACOB
(after a moment) Another grand day tomorrow.

HAROLD clears his throat.

JACOB
Pardon?

HAROLD shakes his head. Silence.

JACOB
(embarrassed) Well, why don't we see what mischief the women are up to?

HAROLD nods. With visible relief both men exit together.

BILL
Tomorrow's off! We've got to tell them, Kathy! And right now!

KATHY
We don't have to call it off.

BILL
What do you mean?

KATHY
You know what I mean.

BILL
You mean you'd get married without having to?

KATHY
I work, you know. I'll be getting a raise in two months, and another six months after that. I'll be making good money by

the time you get into university. I could help put you through. *(slight pause)* I wouldn't be in the way. *(slight pause)* Billy? Don't you even care for me?

BILL

Sure.

KATHY

How much?

Enter HAROLD. During the dialogue he helps himself to another drink from the dining room and crosses to the chesterfield.

BILL

A lot. But I still don't want to get married. I'm not ready. We're too young. Christ, you can't even cook!

KATHY

And you're just a mama's boy!

HAROLD is now seated. KATHY stares at him a moment. Then she smiles.

KATHY

Well, Harold wants me, even if you don't. Don't you, Harold? *(She rises and crosses to the chesterfield, flaunting herself.)*

BILL

Kathy!

KATHY

(to HAROLD) I've seen the way you look at me. *(She drops on the chesterfield beside HAROLD.)* You'd like to hop in the sack with me, wouldn't you? Tell the truth.

BILL

Why are you doing this?

KATHY

You think he's any different than you?

BILL

What do you mean?

KATHY

This make you jealous, Billy? *(She caresses the inside of HAROLD's thigh.)*

BILL

(grabbing her by the wrist) I don't understand you, Kathy.

KATHY

I understand you, Billy. Only too well. Poor trapped Billy.

BILL

I'm not trapped.

KATHY

Aren't you?

BILL

No! I'll call it off!

KATHY

Yes! Why don't you?

BILL

I will!

KATHY

I wouldn't want you to waste your life. I'll bet now you wished you'd never met me, don't you? You wish you'd never touched me. All this trouble because you didn't have the nerve to go to the drugstore!

BILL

Well, why did you let me do it if it wasn't a safe time? Answer me that!

Enter MINNIE, JACOB, and MARY.

MINNIE

Well, kids, you're well off now. More than we got when we started out, heh, Mary? Willard and me didn't have a pot to piss in or a window to t'row it out. *(to JACOB, as she sits)* Where's your eldest? I ain't met him yet.

JACOB

Ben? Oh, he's in his bedroom—*(He glances at MARY who is now sitting in the armchair.)*—studying. He's in university, Minnie. *(He calls to BEN's door.)* Ben, come out. *(slight pause)* And bring your diploma. *(He glances sheepishly at MARY and looks away. MARY shakes her head, amused.)*

Enter BEN, dressed in a sport jacket. He carries his rolled-up diploma tied with a ribbon.

Graduated from Grade T'irteen last night, Minnie. That's Ben. Ben, this is Mrs. Jackson, and that's Harold.

They all nod hello.

MINNIE

(appraising BEN with obvious delight) So this is the best man, heh? Well. Well, well, well. What a fine-looking boy, Jacob. He'll be tall.

JACOB

A little too t'in, Minnie. And not much colour to his face.

MINNIE

What odds? You was a skeleton yourself at his age. Tell you what, Ben. Be over some Saturday night and give you a scrubbing down in the tub. We'll send your father and mother to the pictures. *(to MARY)* Oh, how wicked, maid. Don't mind me, I've got the dirtiest tongue. The t'ings I comes out with. That's what comes of hanging around racetracks and taverns with the likes of the Formaldehyde Kid here. *(slight pause)* You looks like your mother's side of the family, Ben.

JACOB

I kind of t'ought he looked like my side. *(to BEN)* Show Minnie your diploma.

BEN hands the diploma to MINNIE.

MINNIE

(to BEN) Proud father.

BEN

(to JACOB) I thought you didn't have any whiskey?

JACOB

(ignoring BEN and glancing over MINNIE's shoulder as she reads the diploma) He got honours all the way t'rough high school, Minnie. He got a scholarship.

MINNIE

Where'd he get his brains to? *(embarrassed silence–to BEN)* Told you you look like your mother's side. *(She hands back the diploma, rises, and hands her glass to JACOB.)* Next round less ginger ale, Jacob. Gives me gas. *(crossing to the record player)* And I'd hate to start cracking off around Father Douglas. *(She puts on a record– 'Moonglow' theme from 'Picnic'.)* What a face he's got on him, already, the priest. Pinched little mouth. You'd t'ink he just opened the Song of Solomon and found a fart pressed between the pages like a rose. *(She starts to move slowly to the music.)*

KATHY

Mother, do you have to?

MINNIE

Do I have to what, sister?

KATHY

Make a fool of yourself.

MINNIE

Listen to who's talking! *(slight pause)* I'd dance with Harold except the only tune he knows is the Death March. And the only step he knows is the foxtrot. Imagine foxtrotting to the Death March. *(to JACOB)* Jacob, you was a one for dancing years ago. Wasn't he, Mary?

MARY

He still is, Minnie.

MINNIE

Did he ever tell you how I first got to go out with him?

MARY

I don't believe he did.

MINNIE

He didn't? Well, remember Georgie Bishop? He took me out one night—to the Salvation Army dance at Bay Roberts. It was in the wintertime, and cold as a nun's tit. I saw Jacob there, hanging about, and now and then he'd look my way and I'd wink. Oh, I was some brazen.

JACOB

I t'ought you had somet'ing in your eye, Minnie.

MINNIE

Yes, boy, the same as was in yours—the devil!... To make a long story short, Mary, when it come time to go home, Georgie and me went outside where his horse and sled was hitched to the post. He'd tied it fast with a knot, and do you know what this bugger had gone and done?

JACOB

Now don't tell that, Minnie.

MINNIE

Pissed on the knot! He had, maid. A ball of ice as big as me fist. And who do you suppose walks up large as life and offers to drive me home in his sled? *(pause)* Poor Georgie. The last I remembers of him he was cursing the dirty son-of-a-bitch that had done it and was stabbing away at the knot with his jack-knife! *(She notices BEN's amused reaction to her story.)* Come dance with me, Ben. Don't be shy. Come on. If I'm not mistaken, you've got the devil in your eye, too. Just like your father. *(She puts BEN's arm around her waist and they dance.)* Look, Harold. You might learn a t'ing or two. *(She presses close against BEN.)* Mmm. You know, Jacob, this is no longer a little boy. He's coming of age.

KATHY
Mother, you're **dirty**.

MINNIE
How fast you've grown, Ben. How tall and straight. Do you want to hear a funny one? I could have been your mother. Imagine. But your grandfather—Jacob's father—put his foot down. I was a Catholic, and that was that in no uncertain terms. Wasn't it, Jacob? *(slight pause)* So I married Willard. . . .

They break apart.

MINNIE
(to JACOB, as she sits) Ah well, boy, I suppose it all worked out for the best. Just t'ink, Jacob—if you had married me it might have been you Harold pumped full of fluids.

JACOB
That it might, Minnie. That it might.

MINNIE
But you can't help marvel at the way t'ings work out. Makes you wonder sometimes.

JACOB
(Turns off music.) What's that, Minnie?

MINNIE
(slyly) Your son marrying my daughter and turning Catholic in the bargain. Serves you right, you old bugger. The last laugh's

on you. **And** your poor old father.

JACOB

You'm not still carrying that grudge around inside you, is you? I'm getting a fine girl in the family. That's the way I looks at it.

MINNIE

(*rising to help herself to another drink*) I don't mind telling you, Jacob, I've had my hands full with **that** one. Not a moment's peace since the day poor Willard died. She was kind of stuck on her father, you know. Jesus, boy, she won't even speak to Harold. Won't let him give her away tomorrow, will you, sister? Her uncle's doing that. Oh, she snaps me head off if I as much as makes a suggestion. T'inks she knows it all. And now look. All I can say is I'm glad her father ain't alive, this night.

JACOB

Now, Minnie, you knows you don't mean all that. Own up to it.

MINNIE

Oh, I means it, boy, and more. T'ank God it's only the second month. At least she don't show yet. If she's anyt'ing like me, she'll have a bad time. Well, a little pain'll teach her a good lesson.

KATHY

I wish you wouldn't talk about me like that, Mother.

MINNIE

Like what?

KATHY

Like I was invisible. I don't like it; I've told you before.

JACOB

Now, now, Kathy.

MINNIE

Listen to her, will you? Invisible. Sister, you may soon wish you **was** invisible, when the girls from work start counting back on the office calendar.

KATHY

Let them count!

MINNIE

See, Jacob? See what I'm up against? No shame!

JACOB

Minnie, let's not have any hard feelings. It's most time for church. I'll get the coats.

MARY

Yes, do.

JACOB gets MINNIE's and MARY's coats.

MINNIE

(crossing to BEN) You don't know, Mary, how fortunate you is having sons. That's the biggest letdown of me life, not having a boy.... We couldn't have any but the one... *(bitterly)* and that had to be the bitch of the litter. How I curse the day. A boy like this must be a constant joy, Mary.

MARY

And a tribulation, maid.

MINNIE

Yes, but look at all the worry a daughter brings. *(as JACOB helps her into her coat)* This is the kind of fix she can get herself into.

KATHY

Mother, I just asked you not to.

BILL

Tell her, Kathy.

MINNIE

And then to top it off who gets the bill for the wedding? Oh, it's just dandy having a daughter, just dandy. I could wring her neck.

BILL

Kathy.

KATHY

(to BILL) You tell her.

MINNIE

If I had my own way I know what I'd do with all the bitches at birth. I'd do with them exactly what we did back home with the kittens—

KATHY

I'm not pregnant!

MINNIE

What?

KATHY

(bitterly) You heard me. I'm not pregnant.

MINNIE

What do you mean you're not? You are so, unless you've done somet'ing to yourself. . . .

KATHY

I didn't.

MARY

Kathy.

MINNIE

I took you to the doctor myself. I was in his office. Why in hell do you suppose you're getting married tomorrow, if it's not because you're having a baby?

74

KATHY
(*turning to MARY*) Mrs. Mercer, I had a miscarriage. . . .

MINNIE
A miscarriage . . .

MARY
When, Kathy? (*She puts her arms around KATHY.*)

KATHY
This morning. I went to the doctor. There's no mistake. And I didn't do anything to myself, Mother.

MINNIE
(*quietly*) Did I say you did, sister?

MARY
Sit down, dear. (*She helps KATHY sit—long pause.*) This may not be the right moment to mention it, Minnie, but . . . well, it seems to me t'ings have altered somewhat. (*She looks at BEN.*) T'ings are back to the way they used to be. The youngsters don't need to get married. There's no reason to, now.

Pause. No one moves except HAROLD who raises his glass to drink.

BLACKOUT

ACT TWO

A moment later. As the lights come up, the actors are in the exact positions and attitudes they were in at end of Act One. The tableau dissolves into action.

JACOB
Sit down, Minnie. We've got to talk this out. (*to KATHY*) Can I get you anyt'ing, my dear?

KATHY shakes her head. MINNIE sits.

MINNIE
(slight pause) What time is it getting to be?

BEN
Seven-fifteen.

MINNIE
The priest expects us there sharp at eight. He's got a mass to say at half-past.

MARY
Now wait just a minute. I t'ink you're being hasty, Minnie. The children can please themselves, now, what they wants to do. Maybe they don't want to get married.

JACOB
Mary's right, Minnie. Ask them.

MINNIE
For someone who don't like to butt in, maid, you got a lot to say sometimes. Stay out of it or I might say somet'ing I'm sorry for.

MARY
I can't stay out of it. I wouldn't advise my worst enemy to jump into marriage that young, and neither would you, Minnie. They'd be far better off waiting till Billy finishes university. . . .

MINNIE
Well, maybe **they** can afford to put it off, but **I** sure as hell can't. The invitations are out . . . the cake's bought, and the dress . . . the flowers arranged for . . . the photographer . . . the priest and organist hired . . . the church and banquet hall rented . . . the food—

KATHY
(jumping up) I don't want to get married!

MARY

What?

MINNIE

What? Don't believe her, Mary. She do so. She's got a stack of love comics a mile high. *(to KATHY)* Now you shut your mouth, sister, or I'll shut it for you.

KATHY

I won't.

MINNIE

You knows what'll happen if you backs out now? I'll be made a laughing stock. Is that what you wants, you little bitch?

KATHY

Don't call me a bitch, you old slut!

MARY

Kathy.

MINNIE

(to JACOB) Did you hear that? Why, I'll slap the face right off her! *(She goes after KATHY.)*

JACOB

(keeping MINNIE away from her daughter) All right, now. This is no way to behave. Tonight of all nights!

KATHY

That's what you are, an old cow! He only wants you for your money. *(indicating HAROLD)*

MINNIE

That's a lie.

KATHY

Is it?

MINNIE

That's a lie. Let me at her, Jacob. I'll knock her to kingdom come.

JACOB

Enough, goddamn it! Both of you!

Silence.

That's better. Let's all ca'm down. We could all learn a lesson from Harold here. He's civilized. *(slight pause)* What we need's a drink.

MINNIE

(as JACOB refills the glasses) Imagine. My own flesh and blood, and she's got it in for me. She's never had much use for me, and even less since I took up with Harold here. She'll say anyt'ing to get back at me. Anyt'ing!

JACOB

Kathy's had a bad time of it, Minnie. No doubt she's upset. *(to MARY)* Remember how you was, when we lost our first? Didn't care if she lived or died. Didn't care if she ever laid eyes on me again, she was that down in the dumps. And I'm surprised, Billy. Not once have you come to her defence or spoken a word of comfort. You've got to be more of a man than that.

BEN

Why can't they get married and Billy still go to school?

MARY

(to BEN) Mind your business.

MINNIE

You hear that, Jacob? That's the one with all the brains.

BEN

(to MARY) I'm just trying to help.

MARY

Who? Yourself?

KATHY

I want him to, Mrs. Mercer. He doesn't have to quit school. I like to work. Honest.

MARY

Well, Billy, you're the only one we haven't heard from. What do you say?

JACOB

Ah, what's it matter if he gets married now or after university? He won't do much better than Kathy.

MINNIE

She's a good girl, in spite of what I said about her. A hard worker. She always pays her board sharp. And clean as a whistle.

JACOB

That's settled, then.

MARY

Is it, Billy?

JACOB

For God's sake, Mary.

MARY

He's got a tongue of his own. Let him answer. The poor child can't get a word in edgewise.

JACOB

Stop mothering him. He's a man now. Let him act like one. (*amused*) Besides, he's just getting cold feet. Ain't you, my son?

BEN

Did you get cold feet, Dad?

JACOB

All men do. *(MARY glances at JACOB who nudges her.)* Even the best of us. Billy'll be fine after tomorrow.

MINNIE

T'anks, Jacob. I could kiss you. Now, Harold, wait your turn, and don't be jealous. *(as she crosses to the record player and selects a record)* The mother of the bride and the father of the groom will now have the next dance. With your permission, Mary?

MARY

With my blessing, maid.

JACOB

(glancing at MARY) I don't know whether I'm up to it, Minnie.

MINNIE

Go on, Jacob. You'll be dancing a jig at your own wake.

Music: 'Isle of Newfoundland'. JACOB takes MINNIE in his arms and they dance. BILL goes to KATHY, takes her hand and leads her into the darkened kitchen. They make up.

MINNIE

Ah, Jacob, remember when we'd hug and smooch in the darkest places on the dance floor? The way he stuck to the shadows, Mary, you'd swear he was a bat. Dance with her, Harold. *(indicating MARY)* She won't bite. *(to JACOB)* He's some wonderful dancer, boy. Went to Arthur Murray's. He's awful shy, though.

MARY and HAROLD exchange glances. HAROLD clears his throat.

Ah, boy, Jacob, I'd better give Harold a turn. He'd sit there all night looking anxious. He likes a good foxtrot. Fancies himself Valentino. Come on, Lazarus.

MINNIE and HAROLD dance. JACOB crosses to MARY who is sitting behind dining room table.

JACOB

Dance, Mary?

MARY

You make a good match, the two of you.

JACOB

Mary, I t'ink you'm jealous.

MARY

Don't be foolish. And don't start showing off. That's the next step.

JACOB

'How beautiful are thy feet with shoes, O prince's daughter! The j'ints of thy t'ighs are like jewels, the work of the hands of a cunning workman.

'Thy navel is like a round goblet, which wanteth not liquor: thy belly is like—'

MARY

(sharply) Jacob!

JACOB

'—an heap of wheat set about with lilies.

'Thy two breasts—'

MARY

All right, boy—enough!

JACOB

(sitting) Do you remember, Mary, when you was just a piss-tail maid picking blueberries on the cliffs behind your father's house, your poor knees tattooed from kneeling? Did you ever t'ink for a single minute that one day you'd be the mother of grown-up sons and one of 'em about to start a life of his own?

MARY

No, and that I didn't. In those days I couldn't see no further ahead than you charging down Country Road on your old white horse to whisk me away to the mainland.

JACOB
Any regrets?

MARY
What does you t'ink?

JACOB
Ah, go on with you. *(pause)* The old house seems smaller already, don't it?

MARY
Empty.

MINNIE
(still dancing) Tomorrow's a landmark for us all, Jacob. I lose me only daughter and you lose your two sons. *(JACOB reacts.)* Somehow I don't envy you, boy. I t'ink it'll be harder on you. If I had sons . . .

JACOB crosses quickly to the record player and switches it off.

JACOB
What was that you just said, Minnie? Did I hear you correct? Whose sons?

MINNIE
Yours.

JACOB
Mine? Only one's going.

MINNIE
Didn't anybody tell you?

JACOB
Tell me what? I'm lucky to get the time of day. *(to MARY)* Tell me what?

MARY

Ben's moving in with Bill and Kathy. Taking their spare room.

JACOB

He is like hell!

BEN

I am!

JACOB

You'm not!

BEN

I am!

JACOB

Don't be foolish!

MINNIE

I t'ought he knowed, Mary. I t'ought the kids had told him.

JACOB

No, Minnie, they neglected to mention it. I'm not surprised!

MINNIE

I wouldn't have put me big foot in me mouth otherwise.

JACOB

Why should I know any more what goes on in my own house than the stranger on the street? I'm only his father. I'm not the one they all confides in around this house, I can tell you. I'm just the goddamn old fool. That's all! The goddamn fool.

BEN

I wanted to tell you after the wedding.

JACOB

Yes, you did so.

BEN

I would have sooner, but this is what happens.

JACOB

Oh, so now it's all my fault?

BEN

I didn't say that. Stop twisting what I say.

JACOB

How quick you is to shift the blame, my son. *(to MARY)* How come you to know? He was quick enough to run to you with the news, wasn't he?

MARY

I can't help that.

JACOB

Yes, you can. I'm always the last to find out, and you'm the reason, Mary. You'm the ringleader. The t'ree of you against the one of me.

MARY

And you talks about shifting the blame.

JACOB

Wasn't I the last to find out Billy was getting married? He told you first, but did you come and confide in me? That you didn't. If I hadn't found that bill from Ostranders for Kathy's engagement ring. . . !

BILL

We would have told you . . .

JACOB

A lot of respect you show for your father. A lot of respect. You'm no better than your brother.

MARY

Ca'm down, boy. You're just getting yourself all worked up.

JACOB

I won't ca'm down. Ca'm down. All I ever does is break my
back for their good and comfort, and how is it they repays me?
A slap in the face! *(to BEN)* What did you have in mind to
do, my son? Sneak off with all your belongings, like a t'ief,
while your father was at work?

BEN

Go to hell.

JACOB

What did you say?

BEN

You heard me. I don't have to take shit like that from anyone.
And I don't care who's here!

JACOB takes a threatening step toward his son. MARY steps between.

JACOB

I'll knock your goddamn block off!

MARY

Now just stop it, the both of you! Stop it!

MINNIE

I'd never have gotten away with that from my father. He'd have
tanned me good.

MARY

And Minnie—mind your own business. This is none of your
concern.

JACOB

Talking like that to his own father . . .

BEN

And if you ever hit me again. . . !

JACOB

I'll hit you in two seconds flat, if you carries on. Just keep it up. Don't t'ink for one minute you'm too old yet!

BEN

Come on. Hit me. I'm not scared. Hit me. You'd never see me again!

MARY

(slapping BEN) Shut right up. You're just as bad as he is!

MINNIE

Two of a kind, maid. Two peas in a pod. That's why they don't get on.

JACOB

Why the hell do you suppose we slaved to buy this house, if it wasn't for you two? And now you won't stick around long enough to help pay back a red cent. You'd rather pay rent to a stranger!

BILL

Dad, I'm leaving to get married, in case you forgot.

JACOB

You don't need to. Put it off. Listen to your mother!

BILL

A minute ago you said—

JACOB

Forget a minute ago! This is now!

BEN

He'll have converted for nothing, if he does!

JACOB

You shut your bloody mouth! *(to BILL)* Put it off, my son. There's no hurry. Don't be swayed by Minnie. She's just t'inking of herself. Getting revenge for old hurts.

MINNIE

And you're full of shit, Jacob.

JACOB

You goddamn Catholics, you don't even believe in birth control. Holy Jumping Jesus Christ. The poor young boy'll be saddled with a gang of little ones before he knows it! And all because my poor father hated the Micks!

MINNIE

Come on, sister, we don't need that. Get your coat. You, too, Harold. Let's go, Billy. The priest can't wait on the likes of us.

BILL and KATHY move to go.

JACOB

Don't go, Billy. There's no need!

BILL

First you say one thing, Dad, and then you say something else. Will you please make up your mind! *(to BEN)* Ben, what should I do? Tell me.

BEN

I can't help you, Billy.

KATHY looks at BILL, then runs out, slamming the door.

MARY

(to BILL) Go after her, my son. Now's the time she needs you. We'll see you in church. Go on, now.

BILL

Ben?

BEN
In a minute. I'll see you there.

BILL
Dad?

JACOB turns away. BILL runs out.

MINNIE
I'll take the two kids with me, Mary. See you in a few minutes.

JACOB
You won't see me there tonight, Minnie, and you can count on that. And not tomorrow, either.

MINNIE
That's up to you, Jacob, though I hope you changes your mind for Billy's sake. *(slight pause)* We oughtn't to let our differences interfere with the children. *(slight pause)* Come along, Lazarus. It's time we dragged our backsides to the church.

They exit. Silence. MARY removes her coat, then slowly begins to clear the table. BEN looks over at his father. Finally he speaks.

BEN
Dad . . .

JACOB
What?

BEN
I want to explain. Will you let me?

JACOB
I should t'ink you'd be ashamed to even look at me, let alone open your mouth. *(slight pause)* Well? What is it? I suppose we'm not good enough for you?

BEN
Oh, come on.

JACOB

(to MARY) If you's going to the church, you'd better be off.

BEN

We still have a few minutes

JACOB

(to MARY) And no odds what, I won't go to church. They can do without me.

MARY

Suit yourself. But I'm going. Just don't come back on me afterwards for not coaxing you to.

JACOB

You can walk in that church tonight, feeling the way you does? Oh, you'm some two-faced, Mary.

MARY

Don't you talk. You was quite willing to see Billy go, till it slipped out that Ben was going, too.

JACOB

That's a lie!

MARY

Is it?

JACOB

That's a damn lie!

MARY

I'll call a cab. *(She crosses to the phone, picks up the receiver. To JACOB)* We can't always have it our way. *(She dials and ad libs softly while dialogue continues between father and son.)*

JACOB

A lifetime spent in this house, and he gives us less notice than you would a landlord! And me about to wallpaper his room like a goddamn fool! *(slight pause)* And don't come back broke and starving in a week or two and expect a handout, 'cause the only way you'll get t'rough that door is to break it in! *(slight pause)* You'll never last on your own. You never had to provide for yourself.

BEN

I'll learn.

JACOB

You'll starve.

BEN

All right, I'll starve. And then you can have the satisfaction of being right. *(slight pause)* You're always telling me it's time I got out on my own and grew up.

JACOB

Sure, t'row up in my face what I said in the past!

BEN

Dad, will you listen to me for once? It's not because home's bad, or because I hate you. It's not that. I just want to be independent, that's all. Can't you understand that? *(slight pause)* I had to move out sometime.

JACOB

Was it somet'ing I said? What was it? Tell me. I must have said somet'ing!

BEN

No, it was nothing you said. Will you come off it?

JACOB

Can you imagine what our relatives will say, once they hears? They'll say you left home on account of me.

BEN

Well, who the hell cares?

JACOB

And you any idea what this'll do to your mother? You'm her favourite. (*The last syllable rhymes with 'night'.*)

MARY

Jacob! That's not fair!

JACOB

What odds? It's true, and don't deny it. (*to BEN*) Your mother's always been most fond of you. She even delivered you herself. Did you know that?

MARY

There's no time for family history, Father.

JACOB moves quickly to the mantel and takes the photo album. He is slightly desperate now. He flicks open the album.

JACOB

(*intimately, to BEN*) Look. Look at that one. You could scarcely walk. Clinging for dear life to your mother's knee. (*turning the page*) And look at this. The four of us. Harry Saunders took that of us with my old box camera the day the Germans marched into Paris. (*Turns the photo over.*) There. You'm good with dates. June 14, 1940. Look how lovely your mother looks, my son. No more than ninety pounds when she had you.

MARY

Ninety-one.

JACOB

She was that t'in, you'd swear the wind would carry her off. We never believed we'd have another, after the first died. He was premature. Seven months, and he only lived a few hours.

MARY

Enough of the past, boy.

JACOB

That was some night, the night you was born. Blizzarding to

beat hell. The doctor lived in Bay Roberts, and I had to hitch up the sled—

MARY

He's heard all that.

JACOB

Some woman, your mother. Cut and tied the cord herself. Had you scrubbed to a shine and was washed herself and back in bed, sound asleep, before we showed up.

MARY

Took all the good out of me, too.

JACOB

And wasn't she a picture? She could have passed for her namesake in the stained glass of a Catholic window, she was that radiant.

MARY

Get on with you.

JACOB

Your mother'd never let on, but you can imagine the state she'll be in if you goes. You'm all that's left now, Ben. The last son. *(a whisper)* I t'ink she wishes you'd stay.

MARY

I heard that. Look, you speak for yourself. I've interfered enough for one night.

JACOB

Your mother has always lived just for the two of you.

MARY

(painted) Oh, Jacob.

JACOB

Always.

BEN

Come on, Dad, that's not true.

JACOB

It is so, now. It is so.

MARY

Well, it's not, and don't you say it is. The likes of that!

JACOB

Confess, Mary. I don't count, I've never counted. Not since the day they was born.

BEN

If that's true, Dad, you should be glad to get rid of both of us. Have Mom all to yourself again.

JACOB

Don't be smart.

MARY

Who's the one making all the fuss? Me or you? Answer me that.

JACOB

No, you'd sit by silent and let me do it for you and take all the shit that comes with it. I'm wise to your little games.

MARY

I can't stop him, if he wants to go. I don't like it any more than you do. I can't imagine this house without our two sons. But if what Ben wants is to go, he's got my blessing. I won't stand in his way because I'm scared. And if you can't speak for yourself, don't speak for me. I'm out of it.

JACOB

If he's so dead set on going, he can march out the door this very minute.

MARY

He will not! Don't be foolish!

JACOB

He will so, if I say so!

JACOB charges into BEN's bedroom and returns with a suitcase which he sets on the floor.

There! Pack your belongings right this second, if we'm not good enough for you.

MARY

Ben, don't pay him no mind.

JACOB

I don't want you in this house another minute, if you'm that anxious to be elsewhere. Ingrate!

MARY

If you don't shut your big yap, he just might, and then you'd be in some state.

JACOB

Oh, I would, would I? Well, we'll just see about that. I'll help him pack, if he likes! *(He charges into BEN's bedroom.)*

MARY

Ben, don't talk back to him when he's mad. It only makes it worse, you knows that.

JACOB comes out with a stack of record albums which he hurls violently to the floor.

There. Enough of that goddamn squealing and squawking. Now I can get some peace and quiet after a hard day's work.

BEN

Dad, I think I ought to . . .

JACOB

Don't open your mouth. I don't want to hear another word!

BEN

All right, make a fool of yourself!

JACOB

(to MARY) And that goes for you, too! *(He charges back into the bedroom.)*

BEN

What'll we do, Mom? We got to get out of here. Can't you stop him?

MARY

All you can do, when he gets like this, is let him run down and tire himself out. His poor father was the same. He'd hurl you t'rough the window one minute and brush the glass off you the next.

JACOB comes out with a stack of new shirts still in the cellophane.

JACOB

And look at this, will you? Talk about a sin. I walks around with my ass out, and here's six new shirts never even opened. *(He hurls the shirts on the pile of records.)*

BEN

I don't want to spoil your fun, Dad, but so far all that stuff belongs to Billy.

JACOB stares at the scattered records and shirts, alarmed.

MARY

Now you've done it, boy. Will you sit down now? You're just making a bigger fool of yourself the longer you stands.

JACOB

(Her reproach is all he needs to get back in stride.) Sure, mock me when I'm down. Well, I'll show you who the fool is. We'll just see who has the last laugh! *(He charges into his own bedroom.)*

MARY picks up the records and shirts.

BEN

(pause) I wanted to tell him, Mom, a week ago. I kept putting it off.

MARY

I wish you had, Ben. This mightn't have happened.

BEN

It's all our fault, anyhow.

MARY

What do you mean?

BEN

We've made him feel like an outsider all these years. The three of us. You, me, Billy. It's always been him and us. Always. As long as I can remember.

MARY

Blame your father's temper. He's always had a bad temper. All we done was try our best to avoid it.

BEN

Yeah, but we make it worse. We feed it. We shouldn't shut him out the way we do.

MARY

And what is it you're not saying, that it's my fault somehow? Is that what you t'inks? Say it.

BEN

I didn't say that.

MARY

Your father believes it. He calls me the ringleader.

BEN

Well, you set the example, Mom, a long time ago. When we were little.

MARY

Don't you talk, Ben. You're some one to point fingers. *(slight pause)* Perhaps I did. Perhaps your father's right all along. But you're no little child any longer, and you haven't been for years. You're a man now, and you never followed anyone's example for too long unless you had a mind to. So don't use that excuse.

BEN

I'm not. I'm just as much to blame as anybody. I know that.

MARY

I always tried to keep the peace. And that wasn't always easy in this family, with you and your father at each other's t'roats night and day. And to keep the peace I had to sometimes keep a good many unpleasant facts from your father. Small, simple t'ings, mostly.

BEN

You were just sparing yourself.

MARY

I was doing what I considered the most good! And don't tell me I wasn't. Oh, Ben, you knows yourself what he's like. If you lost five dollars down the sewer, you didn't dare let on. If you did, he'd dance around the room like one leg was on fire and the other had a bee up it. It was just easier that way, not to tell him. Easier on the whole family. Yes, and easier on myself.

BEN

But it wasn't easier when he found out. On him **or** us.

MARY

He didn't always, Ben.

BEN

No, but when he does, like tonight—it's worse!

JACOB enters from the bedroom, slowly, carrying a small cardboard box. He removes the contents of the box—a neatly folded silk dressing-gown—and throws the box to one side.

JACOB

I won't be needing the likes of this. Take it with you. I've got enough old junk cluttering up my closet.

BEN

I don't want it, either.

MARY

He gave you that for your birthday. You've never even worn it.

JACOB

Take it!

He hurls it violently in BEN's face. Then he notices the diploma lying on the table. He grabs it.

MARY

Not the diploma, Jacob! No!

BEN says nothing. He just stares at his father, who stares back the whole time he removes the ribbon, unfolds the diploma, and tears it into two pieces, then four, then eight. He drops the pieces to the floor.

MARY

God help you. This time you've gone too far.

Pause. Then BEN crosses to the suitcase. He picks it up.

BEN

I'll pack. *(He exits into his bedroom.)*

MARY

All right. You satisfied? You've made me feel deeply ashamed tonight, Jacob, the way you treats Ben. I only hopes he forgives you. I don't know if I would, if it was me.

JACOB

I always knowed it would come to this one day. He's always hated me, and don't say he hasn't. Did you see him tonight? I can't so much as lay a hand on his shoulder. He pulls away. His own father, and I can't touch him. All his life long he's done nothing but mock and defy me, and now he's made me turn him out in anger, my own son. *(to MARY, angrily)* And you can bugger off, too, if you don't like it. Don't let me keep you. Just pack your bag and take him with you. Dare say you'd be happier off. I don't give a good goddamn if the whole lot of you deserts me.

MARY

You don't know when to stop, do you? You just don't know when to call a halt. What must I do? Knock you senseless? You'd go on and on until you brought your whole house tumbling down. I suppose it's late in the day to be expecting miracles, but for God's sake, Jacob, control yourself. For once in your life would you just t'ink before you speaks? **Please!** *(slight pause)* I have no sympathy for you. You brought this all on yourself. You wouldn't listen. Well, listen now. Have you ever in your whole life took two minutes out to try and understand him? Have you? Instead of galloping off in all directions? Dredging up old hurts? Why, not five minutes ago he stood on that exact spot and stuck up for you!

JACOB looks at her, surprised, slightly incredulous.

JACOB

Ben did. . . ?

MARY

Yes, Ben did, and don't look so surprised. Now it may be too late, but there are some t'ings that just have to be said, right now, in the open. Sit down and listen. Sit down. *(JACOB sits.)* For twenty years now I've handled the purse strings in this family, and only because you shoved it off on me. I don't like to do it any more than you do. I'm just as bad at it, except you're better with the excuses. (*JACOB rises.*) I'm not finished. Sit down. (*He does—slight pause.*) Last fall you tumbled off our garage roof and sprained your back. You was laid up for six months all told—November to May—without a red cent of Workmen's Compensation, because the accident didn't happen on the job. And I made all the payments as usual—the mortgages, your truck, the groceries, life insurance, the hydro and oilman, your union dues. All that, and more. I took care of it all. And where, Jacob, do you suppose the money came from? You never once asked. Did you ever wonder?

JACOB
Where? From the bank.

MARY
The bank! We didn't have a nickel in the bank. Not after the second month.

JACOB
What is you getting at, Mary?

MARY
Just this. (*She lowers her voice.*) If Ben hadn't got a scholarship, he wouldn't have went to college this fall. He couldn't have afforded to. It was his money that took us over the winter. All those years of working part-time and summers. All of it gone.

JACOB
Ben did that?

MARY
And you says he hates you!

JACOB
I don't want no handouts from him. I'll pay him back every cent of it.

MARY

Shut up. He'll hear you! He never wanted you to know, so don't you dare let on I told you, you hear? He knowed how proud you is, and he knowed you wouldn't want to t'ink you wasn't supporting your family. *(slight pause)* Now, boy, who's got the last laugh? *(MARY takes her coat and puts it on as she crosses to BEN's door.)* Hurry up, Ben. The taxi ought to be here any second.

She turns and looks at JACOB. There is anguish in her face. When she speaks her voice is drained.

I'm tired, Jacob. And you ought to be, too, by all rights. It's time to quit it. A lifetime of this is enough, you and Ben. Declare it an even match for your own sake, boy, if for nothing else. I don't want to see you keep getting the worst of it. You always did and you still do.

Enter BEN, carrying his suitcase.

BEN

(to MARY) Isn't the cab here yet? It's almost eight.

MARY

He'll beep his horn. *(slight pause)* You don't need to take that now, my son. Pick it up later.

BEN

That's okay, Mom. I've got all I want. The rest you can throw out. *(He sits on his suitcase.)*

JACOB

Your mother told me what you done last winter. I—

MARY

(sharply) Jacob!

JACOB

I wants to t'ank you. I'll pay you back.

MARY

You promised you— *(She stops, shakes her head in exasperation.)*

JACOB

(slight pause) I'm sorry what happened here tonight. I wants you to know that. I'll make it up to you. I will.

BEN

(meaning it) It's nothing. Forget it.

MARY

Let him say he's sorry, Ben. He needs to.

JACOB

Maybe I've been wrong. I suppose I ain't been the best of fathers. I couldn't give you all I'd like to. But I've been the best I could under the circumstances.

BEN

Dad.

JACOB

Hear me out, now. We never seen eye to eye in most cases, but we'm still a family. We've got to stick together. All we got in this world is the family—*(He rises.)*—and it's breaking up, Ben. *(slight pause)* Stay for a while longer. For a few more years.

BEN

I can't.

JACOB

You can. Why not?

BEN

I just can't.

JACOB

Spite! You'm just doing this out of of spite!

BEN shakes his head.

Then reconsider . . . like a good boy. Let your brother rent his room to a stranger, if he's that hard up. Don't let him break us up.

The taxi sounds its horn.

> MARY

There's the taxi now.

> JACOB

(desperately) You don't have to go, my son. You knows I never meant what I said before. You'm welcome to stay as long as you likes, and you won't have to pay a cent of rent. *(even more desperately)* Come back afterwards!

> BEN

No, Dad.

> JACOB

Yes, come back. Like a good boy. I never had a choice in my day, Ben. You do.

> BEN

I don't!

> JACOB

You do so! Don't contradict me!

> BEN

What do you know? You don't know the first thing about me, and you don't want to. You don't know how I feel, and you don't give a shit!

> JACOB

In my day we had a duty to—

> BEN

In your day! I'm sick of hearing about your fucking day! This is **my** day, and we're strangers. You know the men you work with better than you do me! Isn't that right? Isn't it?

JACOB

And you treats your friends better than you do me! I know **that** much, I can tell you. A whole lot better! And with more respect. Using language like that in front of your mother!

The taxi honks impatiently. BEN moves to go. JACOB grabs the suitcase.

MARY

Jacob! The taxi's waiting!

JACOB

(to BEN) You'm not taking that suitcase out of this house! Not this blessed day! *(He puts the suitcase down at a distance.)*

MARY

That's okay, Ben. Leave it. You can come back some other time. *(MARY exits.)*

JACOB

He will like hell. Once he goes, that's it. He came with nothing, he'll go with nothing!

BEN

(slight pause) Do you know why I want to be on my own? The real reason?

JACOB

To whore around!

BEN

Because you're not going to stop until there's nothing left of me. It's not the world that wants to devour me, Dad—it's you!

JACOB whips off his belt.

JACOB

(as he brings it down hard on BEN's back) Then go!

BEN instinctively covers his head, crouching a little, unprotesting.

JACOB
(sobbing, as he brings the belt down again and again) Go! Go! Go! Go! Go!

Finally, as JACOB swings again for the sixth time, BEN whirls and grabs the belt from his father's hand. Then with a violent motion he flings it aside.

BEN
You shouldn't have done that, Dad. You shouldn't. *(He exits.)*

Silence. JACOB retrieves his belt. A slight pause.

JACOB
(fiercely striking the chesterfield with his belt) Holy Jumping Jesus Christ!

Silence. MARY enters from the hallway. JACOB begins to put on his belt. He notices MARY.

What's you doing here? Isn't you going? *(He crosses into the dining room and sits at the table.)*

Slowly MARY puts down her purse and enters the dining room, crossing behind JACOB and sitting at the table beside him. She says nothing.

JACOB
(anguished) In the name of Jesus, Mary, whatever possessed you to marry the likes of me over Jerome McKenzie?

MARY says nothing. Pause.

I've never asked you before, but I've always wondered.

Pause.

MARY
It was that day you, me, and Jerome McKenzie was all sitting around my mother's kitchen and in walked my brother Clifford.

He was teaching Grade Six in St. John's that year, and he told of a story that occurred that very morning at school. You've most likely forgotten. A little girl had come into his class with a note from her teacher. She was told to carry the note around to every class in the school and wait till every teacher read it. Clifford did, with the child standing next to him. The note had t'ree words on it: **Don't she smell?** Well, Jacob, boy, when you heard that, you brought your fist down so hard on the tabletop it cracked one of Mother's good saucers, and that's when I knowed Jerome McKenzie hadn't a hope in hell. *(slight pause)* Q.C. or no Q.C.!

Slowly MARY lifts one foot then the other onto the chair in front of her. The lights slowly dim into darkness.

END

New Drama

(General Editor: Brian Parker)

This series aims to encourage the performance of more Canadian plays and to promote the teaching of Canadian drama in high schools, colleges, and universities. It will include anthology volumes grouping together three or four Canadian plays which have a common interest, and also single play volumes of contemporary plays and Quebec plays in translation. Each volume will contain a critical introduction or afterward, with biographical and bibliographical notes to encourage further research.

In print:

For information on forthcoming plays and anthologies, write:

new press educational
56 The Esplanade East
Toronto 1
Ontario